Voices of the
First World War

Jenny Hill

UNDEAD TREE

© Jenny Hill, 2016.

The author asserts her rights under the Copyright, Designs and Patents Act, 1988, to be identified as the author of this work.

Undead Tree Publications
9 Normanby Terrace, Whitby, YO21 3ES, England.

http://www.undeadtree.com

All Rights Reserved.

No part of this publication may be reproduced, stored in a retrieval system, or transmitted in any form or by any means, electronic, mechanical, photocopying, recording or otherwise without the prior written consent of the publisher or a licence permitting copying in the UK issued by the Copyright Licensing Agency Ltd, 90 Tottenham Court Road, London W1P 9HE.

ISBN 978-1-898728-36-8

5 6 7 8 9

Typeset in Garamond by Undead Tree Publications.

Contents

About the Author 5
Foreword 7
Introduction 9
Acknowledgements 12
The House that Jack built 15
Bangkok, 4th August 1914 19
The Moving Finger 21
Exodus 23
Fighting Fit 25
Journal Entry, 10th November 1914 27
Mons 29
Joe Armstrong, Loyal North Lancashire Regiment 31
Silent Night 33
Three Seasons 35
Fright 39
Zeppelin 41
Taken Unawares 43
Embarkation 45
Heard During Listening Patrol on a Snowy Night 47
Canaries' Song 49
Six Men on Leave 51
Inferno 55
Sporting Chances 57
In the Trenches 59
Letters Home 61
Some Sort of Victory 63
Going Over 67

Leviathan	69
Shaving, in the Trenches, Winter 1917	71
Lusitania	73
Leonard Gordon-Davis Remembers	75
Aces High	77
Nurse Bird	81
The "Angel in the House" Goes Forth	85
Passchendaele	87
Unit	89
Through a Glass, Darkly	93
Nursery Rhyme	95
In Your Dreams	99
Salonika, Night on the Mountain	101
Oh Soldier, Soldier, Won't You?	103
Six Happy Christmases	107
Hand Grenades	111
Lifelines	115
Snapshots	117
One Man's Meat	119
The Americans Arrive	121
Concert Party	123
8th August 1918	127
Rumour	129
Peace	133
Thomas Olive's Demobilisation Payment, March 1920	135
Nunc Dimittis	137

About the Author

Jenny Hill's parents were both artists and she grew up in the heady, creative cultural atmosphere of St Ives, Cornwall. Trained as a singer, she specialises in early music and unaccompanied folk, having taught all age groups and conducted choirs. She is an accomplished painter and book illustrator and has decorated harpsichords for Robert Goble & Son, Oxford.

From 2009 Jenny was the Parish Priest of West Buckrose, North Yorkshire (2009-2014) following three years as a curate in mid-Cornwall. Retiring from the Ministry in 2014, she has more time to devote to her writings, which draw upon her other talents. Once active in the Cornish poetry scene, performing her one-woman show at various venues including the St Ives September Festival, she won the 1st and Bert Thomas Memorial Trophies (2001, 2002) and the Jack Evans cup for verse (2002) at the Gorsedh Kernow, and was commissioned to write a poem to mark the Restoration of the Tregaminion Holy Well at Morvah, Cornwall in 2001.

Her books of poetry include *From Other Worlds*, illustrated by herself; *The Courtyard at Feock Vicarage*, a book plus recording of her poems, part of a multimedia project with artist Douglas Hill and Netherlands pianist and composer, Cees Hiep; and *Twelve Haikus* (2001) about St Ives, a limited edition with her own hand-coloured illustrations.

Jenny enjoys gardening, walking and taking photographs. She has one son, Daniel, a computer programmer and bass player, and lives in Whitby, North Yorkshire with her husband, artist Douglas Hill.

in memory of

Lance Corporal

Eric Spencer

22nd Bn., Manchester Regiment

who died on The Somme, 1st July 1916 Age 22

Foreword

by General the Lord Dannatt GCB CBE MC DL

In these four years of centenary commemoration of the First World War, bookshelves have been filled with revisionist histories, television screens with fresh documentaries, newspapers with new academic analysis and the moat of the Tower of London filled with 888,246 ceramic poppies – one for every British and Colonial soldier who died in the war that was supposed to end war. One wonders what more could be thought, said or written about the First World War? Yet Jenny Hill has produced an absolutely gripping anthology of verse which tells again the well-known story, but in a totally different way.

Soldiers who became poets, and poets who became soldiers, have already furnished a much-borrowed and often-read library of verse, but Jenny Hill has done something that verges on the unique. Her forty-nine poems weave a seamless thread, from a shot in Sarajevo to the threshold of the Cenotaph. These poems are her poems, but they tell other people's stories and express the emotions of soldiers, sailors, airmen, nurses and civilians alike who struggled to make sense of the years from 1914 to 1918. Jenny Hill's readers know well the central spine of the First World War narrative but her poems bring to life the hopes and fears, the joys and the tears, of those who lived and fought their way through that terrible time, and a reflection on those for whom one day during that War was their last. Because the voices that inspired the poems are the actual voices of those who experienced these traumatic and turbulent years, they have an authenticity that is undeniable. For those who have served in more recent conflicts there is an instantly recognisable credibility to the poems. *Shaving, in the Trenches, Winter 1917* could have easily been written by a gunner on Mount Igman looking down on Sarajevo in 1995 as it was by a gunner, perhaps at Passchendaele, in 1917.

And it is the emotional link between Jenny Hill's poems reciting the voices of the First World War to those who have been wounded or bereaved in more recent campaigns that seals the success of this book. Just as the First World War spawned the *Royal British Legion,* so too have the post-9/11 wars spawned *Help for Heroes,* to whom the proceeds of this book are destined. In her work as a Parish Priest, Jenny Hill knows only too well that evil will triumph if not confronted by good. Soldiers, sailors and airmen are not saints but it is their willing duty to put their lives on the line to bring peace out of war and to try to restore order where there is chaos.

Soldiers know too much of the misery of war – rarely is there real glory, more usually an emptiness when the guns fall silent. In Jenny Hill's final poem *Nunc Dimittis* the weary soldier has had enough – but, crucially, he still has hope in his heart:

> ...*Leave the blindfold*
> *of my un-sight, cover my*
> *eyes, until I can believe*
> *there is glory in the light.*

Richard Dannatt,
February 2016.

Introduction

In September 2014 I retired from eight years of employment as a Parish Priest in the Church of England and moved, with my husband, to Whitby. Soon after this, a poster in Whitby's Pannett Park Museum caught my eye. It advertised a writing project set up to commemorate the centenary of the bombardment of Whitby, Scarborough and Hartlepool early in the First World War. At the first meeting I attended, we were played a twenty-minute podcast created by The Imperial War Museum on the subject of Armistice Day, 11th November 1918. I was hooked. I heard voices male and female, survivors of the Great War, talking about their experiences with a frankness and depth of description that could only come from those who had been through the earth-shattering events of those years.

When I got home, I listened again, and wrote. When I discovered there was a vast library of these recordings I listened to another, and wrote again. And so it went on. I'm afraid I was not a very good class member as far as the group's remit was concerned, as I followed my nose thereafter, and decided that having written three poems inspired by the podcast library, I might as well continue and write remaining forty-six. The experience was an emotional rollercoaster. Although one or two of the podcasts offered some levity, such as *Wartime Leisure and Entertainment* and *Sport in War*, most were sobering, and some harrowing in the extreme. Some of the speakers had more to say in a variety of areas than others, and by the time I was halfway through the series I was already beginning to recognise individuals, their ways of telling a story, and their unique attitudes to life. By the time I had finished, just over a year later, I felt I was saying goodbye to friends.

From quite a young age, I'd been touched by the films and photographs I had seen of the First World War, and I remember as a child being told by my maternal grandmother of the death of her much-loved elder brother, Eric. He had been employed as a boilermaker at the start of the war, which was a reserved occupation; he had no need to volunteer for the front line, but like many others at the time, joined up. As often happens in childhood, these memories disappear, only to re-surface when events prompt them. This one re-surfaced for me as I was writing about the Battle of the Somme, and propelled me to search out my great-uncle's war record on the internet, to discover that he had been killed on the very day that I was writing the poem, 1st July, the first day of the Battle of the Somme.

While I was in the process of writing, a friend asked me a question which made me think carefully about the project. The question was: "Why are you writing more poems about the First World War when there are already so many by writers such as Rupert Brooke, Robert Graves and Wilfred Owen?" After some consideration I was able to voice my reasons. I certainly wasn't trying to reproduce what they had set down; they had written from their particular experiences as accomplished poets in a way that could only be said in their own words. What I felt I was doing was making poetry from the voices of those who may never have had the chance or the inclination to do so. I have tried to be as faithful and true to the experiences they have recounted as

I possibly could, and let the voices speak for themselves. In some cases I have used actual names such as in *Leonard Gordon-Davies Remembers* and *Fright*. In some I have quoted particularly colourful or memorable phrases, and in some cases paraphrased them. In yet others I have tried to paint the mood of the events drawn by an array of speakers.

All of the poems are written from the Allied (and mostly British) point of view, as this is what is largely contained within the podcasts. So much material is presented therein, that inevitably I had to make choices. I have tried not to demonise the enemy, nor to use jingoistic language, as both of these points are virtually absent in the recordings. The exception to this is in *Concert Party*, which is a parody of a song as it might have been created in the trenches.

What I hope the poems do, in addition to giving my perspective on the lives of the men and women I have encountered here, and the tragedy of the years 1914-1918, is to speak into current world situations, those tragedies of life that are still with us: war and its consequences, post-traumatic stress, food shortages and the plight of refugees being some of those issues. They are, I hope, a historical document and also a signpost.

Jenny Hill,
Whitby, January 2016.

Acknowledgements

My thanks to Christina Lewis from the *Remember Scarborough* WW1 Centenary project for her early encouragement to pursue my idea; to the Whitby Writers Group and its Poetry Group offshoot, whose sympathetic feedback gave me the courage to perform major surgery on many of the poems on repeated occasions; to General the Lord Dannatt GCB CBE MC DL for his gracious foreword; finally to Ian Clark of Undead Tree Publications, for his meticulous and patient preparation of the manuscript and inspired artwork.

Jenny Hill.

The House that Jack built

Podcast 1: The Shot that led to War

This is the house that Jack built.

This is the shot that rang through the world
that shattered the house that Jack built.

This is the man with the hurt in his eyes
who fired the shot that rang through the world
that shattered the house that Jack built.

This is his hero
who spurned the man with the hurt in his eyes
that fired the shot that rang through the world
that shattered the house that Jack built.

This is the school
which spurred the assassin to search for the hero
that spurned the man with the hurt in his eyes
that fired the shot that rang through the world
that shattered the house that Jack built.

This is the brother
who paid for the schooling
that spurred the assassin to search for the hero
that spurned the man with the hurt in his eyes
that fired the shot that rang through the world
that shattered the house that Jack built.

...

This is the father
who scratched a poor living
to nourish the brother that paid for the schooling
that spurred the assassin to search for the hero
that spurned the man with the hurt in his eyes
that fired the shot that rang through the world
that shattered the house that Jack built.

This is the mother
who buried six children
who wept with the father that scratched a poor living
that nourished the brother that paid for the schooling
that spurred the assassin to search for the hero
that spurned the man with the hurt in his eyes
that fired the shot that rang through the world
that shattered the house that Jack built.

This is the priest
who named the child Gabriel
to solace the mother that buried six children
that wept with the father who scratched a poor living
that nourished the brother that paid for the schooling
that spurred the assassin to search for the hero
that spurned the man with the hurt in his eyes
that fired the shot that rang through the world
that shattered the house that Jack built.

This is the baby
who struggled to live
to be blessed by the priest that named the child Gabriel
that solaced the mother that buried six children
that wept with the father that scratched a poor living
that nourished the brother that paid for the schooling
that spurred the assassin to search for the hero
that spurned the man with the hurt in his eyes
that fired the shot that rang through the world
that shattered the house that Jack built.

. . .

Welcome.

Bangkok, 4th August 1914

Podcast 2: Outbreak – 4th August 1914

The annual expatriates' tournament:
heads down, a steaming centipede
of salty bodies, legs mashed
with mud, blood and strong words;
a broken nose, bruised ribs,
the rest washed off in time for dinner.

But we play another game that day:
the table: hospital-crisp linen
opens itself for the careless stain;
silver, marshalled proud as a row of medals;
an English, French or German eye
winks back from each charged glass.

A door bangs, loud, like
a warning in the middle of a dream,
and the news throws itself drunkenly
around the room. Unseemly behaviour,
we say, for such an occasion!
The War will begin tomorrow.

The Moving Finger

Podcast 3: Joining Up

The finger points; it follows me about
the town, a digit-mouth, a soundless shout
that beckons round a corner, hooks itself
on to my coat, and hauls me for another bout.

The finger scrawls graffiti on my face
for all to read, 'You're neutered, something less
than man.' It stiffly wags at me; the blood
beneath its nail shows but the smallest trace.

Exodus

Podcast 4: Wrong Place, Wrong Time

Exactly what to take and what to lose?
Safe refuge this no longer, refugee;
we have to leave right now, and you must choose.

We now must travel faster than the news,
and not turn back for one more look to see
exactly what to take, and what to lose.

A coat, a shawl, my child; put on the shoes
that walk in one direction only – we
have got to leave right now, and you must choose.

On things that once meant much you cannot muse;
time is too short for bargaining, agree
exactly what to take and what to lose.

The towns we leave are beaten to a bruise,
No need to lock the door – why take the key?
We have to leave right now, and you must choose.

What comes through choice, and what unseen accrues
makes light or heavy load, evacuee.
Exactly what to take and what to lose?
We have to leave right now, and you must choose.

Fighting Fit

Podcast 5: Training for War

Around we go, to get us fit for war: takes care to get the best from office boys, that used to sit around. We go, to get us fit and loyal to the pack. We're knit to know an order, not request. Around we go, to get us fit, for war takes care to get the best.

Journal Entry, 10th November 1914

Podcast 6: Off to the Front

We rolled out from our tents like horses free
from harness when we heard the news that we
were off. I had, and have my doubts. We left
at five, still dark, without goodbyes – no tears,
no handkerchiefs to wave us off – ten men
in a compartment made for six, with kit,
four biscuits and a tin of bully beef.

The last I saw of England was a house,
one wall a hoarding, on which John Bull bragged:
"The Dawn of Britain's Greatest Glory!" As
I said, I have my doubts. The first to die
was on the quay: a young lance-corporal –
I never knew his name – whose neck
was snapped by half a hundredweight of steel.

We steamed across to France on paddle-boats,
destroyers tearing up and down the coast,
the women tearing buttons from our coats
for keepsakes as they cheered our columns on.
The camp was not so welcoming: the floor
inside the tent was mud, the field
outside the tent was mud, the food was mud.

And now we're moving forward to the Front,
unless the mud eats us along the way;
we look like clay already, since we've dug
and lugged our sunken guns from out the muck.
So will I write again? I have my doubts.

Mons

Podcast 7: Into Battle

I remember our first night,
the summer woodland thick
with sounds. The shells
broke the tree tops,
split with white smoke,
showered on us a thousand
screaming hobs of hell.

We fought well enough,
but not well enough;
retreated like dead men walking.
At every halt, men flung themselves
groundwards where gravity allowed,
as if sleep were a place to suckle.
This leaving withered us.

Joe Armstrong,
Loyal North Lancashire Regiment

Podcast 8: Over by Christmas

A cliché is a lie made palatable:
you taste its sugared coating and you're hooked;
you share it with your friends, it multiplies
until it's at the tip of every tongue.
And here's the morsel everybody nibbled:
"Over by Christmas". When we bit and found
the centre bitter, out there on the Front,
the populace had lost their taste for truth.
And so I keep it to myself, the day
we're ordered *"polish buttons"*, when we shine,
a thousand brassy suns, arising from
a plateau, gunned in turn like fairground ducks,
four hundred down, and only I remain.
I said four hundred, never home again.

Silent Night

Podcast 9: The Christmas Truce

Now, in our present time,
we ask the question carelessly,
as if we had already
thrown the answer away:
Had a good Christmas?
Not in 1914.

That was the year
Wise Men brought
Champagne and chocolates;
Shepherds exchanged
cigarettes and beer;
Angels batted carols
to and fro across enemy lines,
and Peace was born
in a cat's cradle of barbed wire.

Three Seasons

Podcast 10: War in Winter

First came rain. Then came mud, made for
this catch-all cut called trench. Sallow
autumn, finger of winter's claw
pokes, prods and says a brief hallo,
then leaves the soured ground unfallow.
The harvest of a leg, an arm
marks this season of unhallow;
When will our world again be warm?

Then winter bit. It clamped its jaw
ice-toothed; earth that was marshmallow
now rang like steel, its underscore
an electric hum. Our tallow
candles raised a glow so shallow
clothing froze, metal froze to palm,
thought froze. What was there to follow?
When will our world again be warm?

. . .

A season called "hospital": more
like dog-days, limbs corpse-cold, yellow;
crawling for relief, each bleached paw
braced, a scream you had to swallow.
A barking pack; each bedfellow,
mad hyenas, laughing as balm,
beats back words they'd like to bellow –
"When will our world again be warm?"

Call us not unseasoned, callow –
we beg this question without qualm:
you, who live in seasons fallow,
when will our world again be warm?

Fright

Podcast 11: War at Sea

I joined the Navy when I was a boy;
I was still a child when the war began.

Alone on watch and numb with fear
I wept stinging tears that no-one saw.

High on the masthead, the ship a toy
in the palm of the sea, I swung towards

waves like cathedrals vaulting to meet me,
to roof me over; other times

alerted by bottles metalled with moonlight
masquerading as enemy submarines.

Sometimes survivors waved us down,
their shouts stubbed out by our engines' thumps.

We laid them in rows, some of them stiff
as death's mean temperature; those

we slid from the deck, let them slip like fish
returning to water, the best we could do.

Five years on, I was still not yet twenty:
the war made men too old for their years.

Zeppelin

Podcast 12: Zeppelins over Britain

A great cheer went up;
gradually, and with a kind of grace
it fell, turning in the air
like a whale re-entering the water,
and landed in our midst.
Beached,
the sky-swimmer that fed our fears
seemed merely a fly-blown corpse.

In slow time

ribs, fins, fiery jaws danced into the dark,
a Pandora's box of fireworks,
playful as the polka.
With each efflorescence came an animal shout –
from us or the creature - was hard to say.
Soon,
the huge carcass was all alight,
a carnival lantern on a moonless night.

Taken Unawares

Podcast 13: Gas attack at Ypres

The day began with a crash of shells,
as most days did, though different this –
so fierce that we ducked and slid for the trench.

Except for me. I shall never know
why I climbed the tree when the others went down;
a miner's canary instinct, no doubt –

or, the sound that escaped from the splitting shell:
it sizzled and spat as it crept and spread
and slicked the ground with its stinking breath.

I climbed to the top; below me a rug
of yellowish green, that fitted so snug
on the camp, every pocket of good air was gone.

The chlorine gas had stalked its prey,
cauterized each lung, each throat, each eye.
The platoon wiped out. Except for me.

Embarkation

Podcast 14: Gallipoli

Landing. We'd scrambled from boats, and hopes were like fishing-lines, cast and taut, but Gallipoli coiled its lasso, roped us in, pulled the noose.

Hemmed-in, the trench was an open sardine-can. We sat for two days, trapped, eating our meals on an unburied corpse, a flesh and blood sofa.

Vacated by dysentery, bowels were un-knitted in skeins, to be coiled as stinking arrangements, in curdled and red-jellied seething latrines. Our

lives became flies; we were dead upon dead, blackened, heaving together, crusting the wounded, still harvesting life from the bodies they blanket.

Leaving. We're cattle sent shit-soiled from market, roped tight on the lighter; ravelled together, we're all that is holding the each of us upright.

Heard During Listening Patrol on a Snowy Night

Podcast 15: Trench Raids

Staccato snaps – brisk, uneven:
(wire cutters clear an opening).

Woollens shushing over snowfall:
(raiders under wire – a handful).

Fabric tears, the wearer curses:
(barbs have caught some khaki trousers).

Cat-paced footfall, poised and cautious:
(enemy trench within raiders' reaches).

Snap of boots on ice, cold leather:
(trench attained and raiders enter).

Bangs – more distant each explosion:
(grenades are thrown to gain possession).

Silence. A cough. The rasp of matches:
(why so quiet? Why aren't they back yet?)

Footsteps finally, hurried whispers;
(frozen raiders found by rescuers).

Canaries' Song

Podcast 16: Munitions

If we had been ticks
on the necks of their dogs,
they would sooner have picked us off
than share their carriage with us –
you could tell by the way they looked:
officers, thinking of the girls they left behind –
Monday's children, a-froth with lace;
"Well, someone's got to do it" –
patronising.

Our yellowness marked us out,
but not as cowards. A man's work,
and singing for our supper
a thing of the past. We were
important for a while.

We worked the screaming lathes,
twelve hour shifts, no cups of tea.
We picked and packed black rocks of TNT,
we rammed explosive into shells,
lined them up on the factory floor,
a nursery of metal pods
like ticks gorged on blood,
awaiting release.

Six Men on Leave

Podcast 17: Home on Leave

Not far from gods, they looked on us back home,
dined on our reputations for a time,
were brown and strong the first days we got leave.
The girls! They clung behind us like a train,
so fine in our dress uniforms, bespoke –
enough to break a heart and shed a tear.

When I got here, my first job was to tear
the clothes from off my back; at home
the sweat and dirt seemed more ingrained, and spoke
of darkness best forgotten for a time.
So used to sleeping hard, I have to train
my limbs to feather beds before I leave.

I had to do the oddest thing on leave:
a knock came on the door – I had to tear
myself out of my solitude, and train,
at the request of total strangers home
on leave, to be best man, in record time,
and witness wedding vows, as each one spoke.

It captured me, the way those women spoke –
not noticed that I'd missed it till on leave.
They walked, a drift of lavender and thyme;
I listened hungrily, and could not tear
myself from English accents, modulating home.
They were my queens, and I the page in train.

...

Beneath Egyptian sun, with camel train
I journeyed into ancient lands, which spoke
of Bible stories, fabled kings, their home
a pyramid. To climb the sphinx on leave
was consolation, when too far to tear
away to Blighty, and be back on time.

Those places so familiar in time
of peace were best to visit not in train,
but on my bike. I could not wait to tear
around the countryside I loved. Each spoke
would frame a picture as it turned, and leave
a moving magic lantern show of home.

They've called our time – it seems we barely spoke –
it sped on train-like. Now we take our leave
for what is but a tear away: our home.

Inferno

Podcast 18: Mesopotamia

We thought that we'd struck lucky when we came –
the sun, the palms, the colours loud that clashed,
the markets ripe with fruit we could not name.

The fights were tame at first. Our Colonel slashed,
he said, a Turk *"like knife through butter"*, soft;
almost embarrassed by the blood we'd splashed.

Like beetles, dug ourselves an undercroft
against the heat; the sun still searched us out
and crisped our skins like seaweed hung aloft.

Sunstroke, malaria and sores, and then a bout
of sandfly fever; some of us would not
see home again, of that there was no doubt.

And no relief, and six weeks passed. We'd got
through our supplies – ate Arab mules and spoiled
porridge, weevils bobbing up the pot.

And no relief. We gradually uncoiled
and showed our underbelly, as our flag
hauled up – white – our cocksure victory foiled.

And then? Six weeks in London on a jag
won't torch those thoughts which cling like filthy rag.

Sporting Chances

Podcast 19: Sport in War

As beautiful a game, as rich a sport
as ever raised a chant or cheer back home.
We left behind each battle-weary thought
propped up against the trench in monochrome.
We etched a pitch in sand instead of loam,
we threw our jackets down to mark the goal –
the only shots we aimed that fed the soul.

We'd lumped the bats and balls and bales and stumps
from school to home, from home to school each term:
to find a level pitch was rare – the humps
and folds more like the skin of pachyderm,
with trees like lazy fielders grown infirm.
We lugged the playing fields of Eton here
in canvas, bags of Thames and green Berkshire.

I swam – the sea my element. I cast
my clothes upon the dazzling sand, struck out
along the Hellespont until, foot-fast
by Sirens I was seized and turned about,
to land as Aphrodite, but without
the shell, the breasts, the cape of curling hair,
my decent drapes left on a beach somewhere.

In the Trenches

Podcast 20: Trench life

The trenches' filthy gums
gape for fresh meat,
their appetite for boots and bodies
bottomless.

Rats arrive, honed to one aim:
to ravage your rations,
feed themselves fat;
chew corpse or living alike.

Hunger gnaws,
food fails to arrive;
sleep fails to arrive,
the night is full of holes.

The lice eat their fill,
most intimate friends,
bloating their pale bodies
with your thin blood.

Fifth, the fever,
the silent visitor,
who sips at your strength
till blood feels like water.

And last,
the most savage
of all that gnaws

is the emptiness.

Letters Home

Podcast 21: News from the Front

Dear Louise, it gives me the greatest joy to
hear the good your trip to the country did. But
really, fancy letting a crow upset you!
Love from the hell-hole.

Thanks, the parcel came – it arrived just four months
since you sent it. Chocolate was melted, sweets were
sticky, insect cream was like gold-dust, my best
luxury item.

Sweetheart, sorry I've not had a chance to write. I've
been court-marshalled, tied to a wheel all weathers.
Wrote some news I shouldn't have told of, never,
in a love letter.

Dearest All, we've had quite a merry Christmas;
met the Germans opposite – talked and joked; we
kicked a ball, we swapped cigarettes and buttons
in between trenches.

Deep regret, we have to inform that Frank is
dead, is drowned, the water now laps his head, the
waving weeds entangle his feet, he drifts with
shoals around Jutland.

Just delete whatever you want to leave un-
said. Field postcards give an all-purpose range of
options: Well. In hospital. Sent to base. Still
waiting your letter.

Some Sort of Victory

Podcast 22: Jutland

The sea is in our blood, we share a history,
our veins awash with salt; she is our mother, and
the ship a wife we kiss and curse in equal measure,
serve with clockwork regularity, and love
a good deal more than ever we'd admit out loud.
We call her names: *Indomitable, Lion, Tiger,
Warspite, Onslaught, Indefatigable,* tease
her when the going's good with *Hercules,
King George* or *Marlborough,* coax with *Galatea.*
She likes a scrap, and we are ready for one too.
The thirty-first of May, far north in Scapa Flow –
the days are long, the short nights pulse with pale
auroras, signalling a code we cannot understand.
We feel that something's in the air, this day we will
accept a gift of life or death not of our choice.
The bugler will awaken Arthur, napping in
the sun with Smithy, up there on the gun turret;
Farmer clamber up the Jacob's ladder, to
unfurl the tangled flag; the shudder of the salvos
beat through Frederick's every bone, while George will note
his own ship shake like jelly, rise and fall because
a thirteen thousand tonner splits and sinks, taking
a thousand sailors with her; Jacky, just sixteen,
will soon decide to stay beside the for'ard gun,
and Hubert will be rescued from the chilling sea;
the chaps will cheer on George's passing ship, their raft
unsaved, surrounded by a glistening flotilla –
fish knocked from the sea, stunned by the guns' boom;

...

J Hazelwood will stagger from his manhole, marvel
that they're still afloat, the bridge in flames, fires
raging in the battery, the upper deck
riddled with shell, and not a lifeboat fit for water;
Arthur will know a night smudged out with smoke,
the dying laid on deck in rows, his chum among them;
Reginald, his voice choked with emotion, will
re-live a watery memorial, the gathering
of what was left, a Service in the Scapa Flow,
a sorrowing of the sea, mourning some sort of victory.

Going Over

Podcast 23: The First Day of the Somme

I shall never get it out of my memory –
they told us to advance slowly, in long lines;
this looks like a sacrifice, I thought.
A hare ran in front, its eyes bulging with fear.

They told us to advance slowly, in long lines,
but we were sitting ducks, walking straight into a death-trap,
like the hare that ran in front, eyes bulging with fear.
Even the rats became hysterical, seeking shelter with us

where we were ducked down: we'd walked straight into a death-trap.
It was a dance of hell, right enough;
some were hysterical as the rats seeking shelter with us.
All I could see was men lying dead.

It was a dance of hell, right enough.
This looks to me like a sacrifice, I thought.
All I could see was men lying dead –
I shall never get it out of my memory.

Leviathan

Podcast 24: Tanks on the Somme

Where were you when I made the
earth tremble, when I laid waste
the foundations of the trench?
Did you see me at my birth,
assembled by the Landships
Committee, a mobile fort,
peripatetic castle?
Did you stare, open-mouthed, when
the tarpaulins were whisked off,
and I was revealed in my
armoured glory? Were you
awed to see this monster crawl
contours, barbed wire, trenches or
mud, unstoppable? Did your
body liquefy with fear
at my inhuman aspect,
when your bullets skittered off
my armour plate like dried peas,
knocking off white hot flakes of
metal that could blind, like snow?
Did you hear my engines roar
like a storm, my tracks rattle
like a mountain avalanche?
I hid well from you the soft
embryos in my belly,
vulnerable as bee grubs
inside the lion's carcass.

Shaving, in the Trenches, Winter 1917

Podcast 25: Winter

...was difficult; in better times it happened
easily, the knife's bright edge explored
the ins and outs, the bone, the fat, the known
and practised territory of my face.
But these are bitter times. The fags long gone,
I pack a Capstan tin with snow; I thaw
it on a candle, lather up in haste,
my stiff hands following the raked field
of the blade's progress, numb to nicks and cuts.
Done, the thickened soapy soup has cooled,
the brush and tin, the blade and bristles fused
in ice, a still-life tableau till next day.
We may have frost-bite, trench foot or exposure,
but still we'll go out looking like a soldier.

Lusitania

Podcast 26: The Submarine War

Sometimes,
the shored-up door of forgetfulness,
as if stormed by an ill wind,
flings open,
and before I lunge for the handle
to slam it shut,
I see this one picture:

a day of such beauty,
the sun shining blandly,
as I tumble towards the water
pearl-blue and soft as hyacinth petals;
while the U-boat,
resting delicately on the sea's skin,
like a pond-skater between the lily pads,
regards our broken ship casually,
as only a dragonfly's discarded sheath,
a thing of no importance.

In that picture of my falling
(for this sensation over-rides the rescue, the escape)
I watch the sea open,
to receive one by one, three funnels,
and hundred by hundred the melée of jumbled bodies,
until the wound is seamlessly closed,
and oil anoints the surface like a black balm.

Leonard Gordon-Davis Remembers

Podcast 27: Arras & Vimy

The men felt they were moving towards victory;
success had given them an air of confidence.
The campaign was well-organised and prepared:
a week's heavy bombardment, a fully-equipped
sortie, all objectives achieved. But it was not
a turning tide, it was a storm that whipped them back
each time they surfaced.

He is old now; when he speaks his voice wavers:
*"We had to occupy a place called Oppy Wood.
We made a frontal attack with desperate fighting,
and a fixed bayonet charge. I've never experienced
anything so ghastly, and I hope I shall eventually
forget it."*

New recruits, they went berserk, went haywire,
the whole lot – it was a case of mass shell shock.

*"The bodies about the place, the filth of the place,
and the smells. When one lives for years in this sort of horror,
with parts of bodies about all over the place,
and groans from the dying, and dead bodies, and how casual
one gets about it; one goes on doing what you're
supposed to do. You become careless about these very
serious things."*

Aces High

Podcast 28: War in the Air

A skeleton of wood, a skin of canvas, this flimsy carapace
an airborne parcel tied with string from nose to tail.
We queued to pit ourselves against her, Lady Luck, though it was plain
not all could win. The chosen few rehearsed some ragged
landings, soon were flying solo – I before the hour
was up – helmet belted round my grinning chin, joystick in hand.

Young pups in a pedigree service, we were picked by hand
for the quick wits on which a flying ace
depends. It was a gentleman's life, with our
nights spent on white sheets, clean from top to tail,
filled with a canteen meal, none of the ragged
chaos of the ground troops, that was plain!

We were the eyes of the Western Front – a plane
spies out the eagle's view. With camera craned above the cockpit, hand
manoeuvring the delicate plate, while ducking ragged
gunfire, face and fingers just within an ace
of freezing, three thousand feet above a Gulliver's tale
of life in miniature, king of the castle for this hour.

We treated dogfights as exciting games, patterned our
hero's aptitude for rapid fire, which could reduce a plane
to shreds in minutes: McCudden could escape a tail-
spin with magician's flourish, and a sleight of hand
that palmed the encounter with a sort of grace,
which must have left them wondering how he'd run them ragged.

...

The day my luck ran out, the engine made a rasping, ragged
sound; it stopped, and there we hung. I thought my hour
had come; the shrapnel hit me like a pick-axe, and my ace
was low. Fingers of warm blood tracked my face, the plane
plunged, the space narrowing between me and eternity, till my hand
found the controls, the drop slowed: I re-live each detail.

Times when gloom descended on the mess, voices would tail
off when the question came: *"Where's George?"*, or *"Tom?"* And so we ragged
each other – wasn't that we didn't care; we had to trick the hand
of fate that clicked her fingers over us, if only for an hour;
cajole the Queen of Spades, smoothed by alcohol's plane,
our clipped accents blurred with scotch on ice.

You may be thrown a head or tail, a joker or an ace,
the timing may be ragged, it may be plain:
Fortune is fickle, the hand depends entirely on the hour.

Nurse Bird

Podcast 29: Wounded

Night on the ward,
when time is kinder.
Her pace
slows from run to walk –
not that it's quiet:

There's the amputee who's lost one leg and
half the other, an arm and an eye;
he beats back his groans by day
with smiles and jests –
at night they break free.

There's the suck and hiss of the gunner's lungs
tattered by gas; the random shouts
of the shell-shocked lad that hang
in the antiseptic air;
the soundless presence of someone bandaged
head to toe, where black tunnels mark
eyes, nose, mouth;
they speak more pain
than could ever be contained in a scream.

Worst is the boy's weeping,
devastating in its pianissimo,
who'd placed his hand on the ground,
topped it with his steel helmet,
pushed a Mills bomb beneath
and pulled out the pin.

. . .

She talks with them at night,
her voice sweetening the dark hours
like a bird before dawn;
they are grateful for food and warmth,
but most for this.

The "Angel in the House" Goes Forth

Podcast 30: Womens' War Services

Sick of metaphors, we wanted life.
Dusting off our moth-eaten feathers,
we angels flew from our houses
over the earth in thousands.
WAACS, WAAFS, WRNS,
Rubys, Ethels and Graces,
cooks, clerks, drivers,
nurses, signallers, storewomen,
munitions workers, telephonists.

Wingless, we could
crank a choked ambulance,
coax the milk from a cow,
clear a forest of trees or
change a car tyre.

The wings, we found after it all,
were quite unfit for further use.

Passchendaele

Podcast 31: Passchendaele

With those boys too young
to look Death in the face,
Death took another approach.

Abandoning the usual methods –
guns,
bombs,
bayonets,
land mines –
Death crawled underfoot.

God's good earth
became a monster,
its viscous maw
sucking into itself
horses, mules,
ordnance, even tanks
in its merciless search
for youthful flesh.

The trees,
once the lungs of the earth,
stumps now,
became signposts
to a crucifixion,
a Passion without a Last Supper,
with no decent burial
and with no return.

Unit

Podcast 32: Gunners

A team of eight operated
each gun, and had a specific
role; the first was the sergeant-
in-charge: *"artillery pieces are
extremely cumbersome, getting
bogged down in soft ground.
In Basra, twenty-two horses
were needed to haul out one gun."*

Two, the limber-gunner opened
and closed the breech when in action,
also serviced the gun: *"The noise
is beyond imagining. Shells
that explode not on the ground, but
in a tree, make a tremendous
roar — explosions of colour — blue,
red, yellow, orange, like fireworks."*

Number three, the gun-layer, who
aimed the gun, and needed precise
co-ordinates on the target: *"Howitzers
fire upwards in a curved trajectory,
going up like a lobbed tennis
ball, where the shell almost pauses,
turns like a dancer in mid-air,
then gathers speed as it descends."*

...

The other five were ammunition
numbers; often they had to manage
with less: *"Shells are very heavy.
We each had a saddle contraption
to hang round our necks, with pockets
for shells, made for pre-war recruits –
six footers – useless if you were
short. They didn't think to change them."*

Through a Glass, Darkly

Podcast 33: Shell Shock

Who are you – what are you – weren't you here yesterday?
You look slightly familiar – I feel I should know;
but thoughts run away, silver-fast beads of mercury,
and those hands, made of paper, of tissue, let go.

You look slightly familiar – I feel I should know,
yet your eyes, like a death mask, eat darkness like Sheol,
and those hands made of paper, of tissue, let go
as what holds this together begins to unroll.

Yet your eyes, like a death-mask, eat darkness like Sheol,
seeing bodies as marionettes torn apart
as what holds this together begins to unroll,
and you're re-made a monster, botched-up without chart,

seeing bodies as marionettes torn apart.
You could pull out those thoughts from that head and re-wind,
but you're re-made a monster, botched up without chart,
and the thing they've put in there just isn't a mind.

You could pull out those thoughts from that head and re-wind,
but thoughts run away, silver-fast beads of mercury,
and the thing they've put in there just isn't a mind.
Who are you – what are you – weren't you here yesterday?

Nursery Rhyme

Podcast 34: Animals in War

Chorus:
*Rufus and Kitty and
Jackie and Jen;
Jacko and Dublin and
mule forty-one;
mascot and messenger,
load-bearer, life-saver,
worker and carrier,
companion and friend.*

Born to be worker,
bred for the plough,
shoulders like Hercules,
where are you now?
Turning the sod no more,
marking the field's contour,
seagulls behind, before,
where are you now?

Rufus and Kitty......

Freedom of hills, high
over the sea,
grey-feathered messenger,
where can you be?

...

Mounting the blue no more,
facing the cannon's roar,
your safe return unsure,
where can you be?

*Rufus and Kitty and
Jackie and Jen;
Jacko and Dublin and
mule forty-one;
mascot and messenger,
load-bearer, life-saver,
worker and carrier,
companion and friend.*

Creature so trusting,
trained to the gun,
first friend of humankind,
what have we done?
Sent you to fight our war,
to end all war for sure!
carry the can once more,
what have we done?

Rufus and Kitty......

The animals named in the chorus were working horses and mules, mascots and pets transported to the Front Line. Mule forty-one saved a column of troops from disaster when, sensing danger, he refused to move forward on to a bridge. The bridge was later found to have had the centre bombed away.

In Your Dreams

Podcast 35: Life on the Home Front

Even now they dream of food;
the hunger imprinted
on their tongues
has left their voices
thin, flat, cold.

They re-live early mornings,
their pale, rumpled bodies
forming the day's grey queues,
latched like leeches
on each shop doorway.

Their dreams taste of oranges,
smell of toast thick with lard,
stuff that melts in rivers on their lips,
crackles like searing meat-fat.
Rumours of food settle like flies
on their sleeping ears;
sounds that sizzle with an 's' –
sugar, steak, sausages,
stews bathed in rich juices –
feasts with which to be anointed,
baptized in,
wedded to.
Food to die for.

Salonika, Night on the Mountain
Podcast 36: The Wider War

My feet, I believe, have evolved into eyes,
sensitized to the nights when we journey, climbing;
I've pit-pony eyes, turned in on my soul.

The going is slow, we grope along goat paths,
and stones rattle down to unknowable depths;
my feet, I believe, have evolved into eyes.

Lights flicker distantly, never get nearer –
frail Jack-o'-lanterns, nocturnal mirages?
I've pit-pony eyes, turned in on my soul.

At seven thousand feet the cold is unbearable –
may freeze my blood and muddle the way
my feet, I believe, have evolved into eyes,

so I, like the mule whose scream split the night
will slip from a ledge, heard but unseen, for
I've pit-pony eyes, turned in on my soul.

I visualize no promised land at the end
of this exodus; my transfiguration is this:
my feet, I believe, have evolved into eyes,
I've pit-pony eyes, turned in on my soul.

Oh Soldier, Soldier, Won't You?

Podcast 37: Conscientious Objectors

They stripped him of his own clothes,
placed a uniform beside,
"You've got to put it on," they said,
"then you may come inside."

The month it was November, mist
was crawling grey and chill,
but he, half naked, did not move;
the uniform too lay still.

The story flew around the camp,
and people came to stare
at the man who sat by a pile of clothes
that he refused to wear.

They called out words of encouragement:
"Stick to it boy!" they'd shout,
"stick to it if it kills you, lad,
you've already got less than nowt!"

The major was ready for stand-off;
"Take uniform and tent
and leave him upon the cliff-top
until his stamina's spent.

...

"And roll up the walls of his tent, to let
The wind off the sea wander in
to weaken the soul of the man, who thinks
that to kill a German's a sin.

"And make sure no-one approaches him
until he's dressed like a man.
He can sit and freeze in his singlet and pants
till he deigns to join the clan."

He sat there a day, and he sat there two,
he sat there three and more,
he sat at his tent-pole, clothes at his side,
unashamed of what he wore.

The tenth day came when the doctors arrived,
and carried him to the sick bay;
rigid with cold, starved to the bone,
the uniform still where it lay.

Six Happy Christmases

Podcast 38: Christmas at War

It was my happiest time! I'd save each piece
of useful cloth, stiff card – just couldn't wait
to fix bright stars against the dark blue drop;
to prop up cottages, then spread a sea
of cotton wool on trees. The men around
the ward would rest their eyes there and be still.

For army men it was tradition still
to give the rank and file a rest; each piece
of work was done by officers, so round
came breakfast, lunch and tea – they had to wait
on us on Christmas Day, make sure to see
we'd smokes and beer. We savoured every drop!

I had pea soup for Christmas, each last drop
was licked; potatoes, boiled, canned beef; I still
remember every lovely mouthful. Sea
was coming in the gun-ports, not a piece
of furniture, but so much worth the wait:
tastes better with salt water washing round!

...

"Cherry Whiskey" is what I'm called: they round
on me since Christmas — drank the final drop —
the Brigadier's special; couldn't wait!
We'd propped ourselves against a wall, quite still,
and supped the lot, until a sort of peace
washed round us, like a cherry-flavoured sea.

We struck bad weather one Christmas out at sea.
The ratings had to have their fun, so round
they dragged the piano, lashed it with a piece
of rope up to a stanchion. But the drop
and swell would not allow the piano to be still:
we chased her round the deck, all shouting *"Wait!"*

It was a starlit night. I had to wait
while wounded soldiers left my van, and see
them off for treatment. Lightly injured, still
able to walk, they sang their way around
the winding hills — carols — each note a drop
of something pure and clear you might call peace.

If we could make Time wait a whole year round,
and from one Christmas see the next one drop
beside it, we might still hold on to peace.

Hand Grenades

Podcast 39: Weapons of War

The Jam Tin Grenade was hand-made
in the trenches like this: you put
gunpowder in the empty tin,
then a layer of clay, attached
the detonator to a length
of fuse wire, shoved it through the clay,
filled the top half with nuts, bolts, bits
of scrap iron; threaded the fuse
through a prepared hole in the lid,
then taped the lid on securely.

Cricket Ball Grenades were not made
of cricket balls, but cast iron.
Also called Hand Bombs, they were filled
with ammonal. The waterproof top
was released by a brassard, which
revealed the fuse. The lighter was
struck and the fuse lit. You held on
and counted to five before throwing.

German Stick Grenades were much feared,
as they were highly efficient.
Light and easy to carry, they
could be thrown a long way. A stick

...

attached to a canister, filled
with explosive, they contained
light pieces of metal, which would
fracture into small, sharp shrapnel,
travelling up to fifty yards.

Mills Bombs: hand-sized but effective,
they looked like little pineapples –
the noise they made was deafening.
A narrow strip of metal fixed
the detonating handle; once
you let go of it, a small spring
hit down on the fuse, which gave you
seven seconds, then it went off.
The metal fragmented – pieces
roughly the size of a thumb nail.

Lifelines

Podcast 40: The Logistics of War

(May be read in any direction, backwards, forwards, repetitions *ad lib*.)

The palm of your hand, a map,

hazard of lines and creases, your body's

memory; a tangle of branching networks –

tracks, roads, lanes, by-ways, ginnels.

Those were our pathways; we were

blood that flowed through the veins,

air that inflated the lungs. Night and day,
                                                we tracked,
it was get what rest you could. Logistics -
                                                            us lorry drivers,
though not always logical: ship to shore,
                                                                   not two-a-penny!
to buses, trains, lorries, horses, mules and
                                                               Prized, too;
motorcycles, even feet. People, fuel, food,
                                                                    our chariots
ammunition, clothes, wounded, messages,
   dumps,   without
      like your bowels, need to be kept moving.
  feeding   windscreen,
        A continuous slow flow of trains,
greedy guns,   dispatch riders   solid tyred
        horses with limbered wagons,
our nightly   on motorbikes,
        London buses in columns,
trawl   buzzing about
               carrying troops, compacted
to fetch   wounded men   like flies,
                      to field hospitals,
bombs,   like pilchards   to collect
                      pigeon lofts.
ammo,   packed on   information,
                    Breakdowns,
small   roofless   numbers -
                   confusion,
arms   flat-bed   casualties,
                 wheels in
         trains,   effects of
                mud, just
        rumbling   shelling
               getting on
        mile on
               with it.
        mile
               Life-

               lines

Snapshots

Podcast 41: The German Spring Offensive

All communications broken, nothing comes back;
messages hang, unspoken. Shells answer back.

....

The fog betrays us: the enemy that we faced
has crept up behind, is poking us in the back.

....

Five hours of shelling – noses bleed with the impact.
Then silence unbroken before hearing comes back.

....

Mist lifts like curtains on a mass of men marching –
as football crowds might betoken, returning back.

....

The blast threw us down from the fire step; we gather
his limbs, bloodied, soaking, but cannot join them back.

....

Marching, a prisoner, I hear *"Brave Englander,
brave!"* My German guard has spoken, he pats my back.

....

Dribs and drabbles of leftovers, our line a back
of loose, disjointed bones; heartbroken, we move back.

One Man's Meat

Podcast 42: Prisoners of War

Cold dawn cast us off to each day's drudgery, the dusk dragged us back;
already enfeebled by years of war, our bodies begged for nectar, ambrosia.
Give us this day our daily bread: one small loaf shared between three,
potato meal mainly, a mean thing, no miracle of multiplication.

Each day we woke weaker, limbs less obedient to the workings of our wills.
As rations reduced further, our revulsions grew slimmer, for
one day we discovered, clustered on a tree, on the morning-damp bark,
crustaceans, bubbled on the willow branch, a crust crying to be culled.

We harvested our manna, hid it till evening. We picked and pocketed
                                                                     [prickling nettles,
dropped the lot in a pot. It slopped, snails and nettles, a witches' broth,
the final product a brownish paté, our patented gentleman's relish.
We spread it on bread, and thought it a paste quite beyond taste.

The Americans Arrive

Podcast 43: Arrival of the American Troops

The Englishman Speaks...

When you first arrived in France,
we would gather by the road, if duty allowed,
to watch your battalions swing by.
You were fresh, strong, plump
and new. You waved, laughed,
and shouted to our boys –
a bit full of yourselves,
but we were pleased to see you;
for we were empty, by then.
We'd grin back, masking
the wordless question: *"Do they know?
Do they really know?"*

The American Speaks...

When we marched through the towns
we felt like poured champagne,
the French delirious with joy.
The trenches were another matter:
we were incredulous –
*"Buried in these rat holes for how long?
Three years already?"* We wanted out,
to do some damage, get done,
get back home. We got there in the end,
fought in the woods
like our fathers on the frontier;
made an honest job of it, and turned the tide.

Concert Party

Podcast 44: Wartime Leisure & Entertainment

(To the Tune of "Keep the Home Fires Burning")

Bring your pack of Woodbines,
dodge past all the landmines,
roll up to the barn, dress
circle seats for one and all!
Even though they're straw bales,
the entertainers all males,
for an hour you can enjoy
some good old Music Hall.

Every act's a good 'un,
though they're mostly homespun,
not afraid to get on stage
our own Lieutenant B;
prancing with his hanky
he looked a proper nancy,
bows and bells and finer calves
I think you'll never see.

Then those sweet high kickers,
you could see their tonsils –
what a disappointment
that they're much the same as ours!
And a ballerina,
more like Len than Lena;
for the laughs she's given us
she sure deserves some flowers.

...

Little Harry Lauder,
voice like a marauder,
standing on his orange-box
he sang with all his might;
gave him such a send-off –
nearly took the roof off,
kept the home fires burning
in our hearts throughout the night.

8th August 1918

Podcast 45: The Beginning of the End

Dawn, the eighth of August, a surprise
attack – a change of tactics; for we knew
(just as a long-wed couple may surmise

each other's moves) the signs that a clash was due.
This time we caught them unprepared: our troops
were leapfrogged forwards, each advance a few

miles won. Like charging bulls, the tanks stamped loops
of bristling wire where we could walk, like roads.
We walked in, they walked out in sorry groups.

Each inch we earned proved doggedness erodes;
this forging forward was enough to send
a shiver of excitement like electrodes

spinewards, sensing the course where this would tend,
these wastes of war's wrecked days were soon to end.

Rumour

Podcast 46: The Allied Advance to Victory

There's a fellow in the army called
Rumour – travels light,
doesn't waste his words;
told us we'd taken Lille,
Le Cateau, Selle,
Mormal, Pompelle,
Sambre-Oise.
He'd travelled far,
seen the Ottomans throw in the towel,
Bulgaria backtrack,
Italy wriggle her toes again.

He rallied us through the last rounds,
made sure we knew
of their sagging morale,
dwindling supplies,
exhaustion, starvation;
how they tripped up on their retreat
like backwards-moving clock hands,
too fast to keep in check.

Rumour warned us, though,
that the winding-up
would not come easy.
I can tell you of some
who walked behind
a wall of fire
and did not come out.
To us, they were the saddest –
within a hair's breadth of peace.

...

As the hands on our CO's watch touched eleven, he snapped it shut.
"I wonder", he said,
"what we shall all do next?"

Peace

Podcast 47: Armistice

They say we are at peace –
they made a date, a time for it.
Peace was imposed on us,
as war was imposed on us,
it was no matter of choice.

I am not at peace.
Peace is like a falling –
down, down the gaping lift-shaft
into the black void, leaving
your guts hanging there.

I could have stolen peace;
climbed alone from the trench,
walked towards the blind cannon's eye,
into the silence of the shelling.
I would have known where I was.

Thomas Olive's Demobilisation Payment, March 1920

Podcast 48: Homecoming

Balance due to the soldier
on the date of arrival
at the dispersal station:
two pounds and eighteen shillings.

Twenty-eight days furlough at
eight and twopence a day makes
eleven pounds, eight shillings
and sevenpence – sorry, eight.

Twenty-eight days of ration
allowance at two shillings
and a penny is two pounds,
eleven shillings fourpence.

The allowance for plain clothes
is two pounds, twelve shillings and
fourpence. Total: nineteen pounds,
eighteen shillings and fourpence.

Nunc Dimittis

        God, how I'm thirsty,
        wrung out; a sponge
        squeezed drop by drop
        beyond dryness; I am
        a framework of holes.
Let me go quietly, for my eyes have seen too much;
ask me no more, ask no more of me. Salvation? Yes,
seen in the faces of people — ordinary, exceptional;
        but the clenched hand
        of war will not unlock its
        fingers, will not set me
        free. Leave the blindfold
        of my un-sight, cover my
        eyes, until I can believe
        there is glory in the light.

www.ingramcontent.com/pod-product-compliance
Lightning Source LLC
Chambersburg PA
CBHW070500100426
42743CB00010B/1704